Pastorals
I Timothy, II Timothy, Titus

Bible Study Workbook

Paul C. Jones, PhD

WESTBOW
PRESS
A DIVISION OF THOMAS NELSON
& ZONDERVAN

Scripture taken from the *Holy Bible, New International Version.*® Copyright © 1973, 1978, 1984 by International Bible Society. Used by permission of Zondervan Publishing House. All rights reserved.

Life Application Bible copyright © 1988, 1989, 1990, 1991 by Tyndale House Publishers Inc., Wheaton, IL 60189. All rights reserved.

WestBow Press books may be ordered through booksellers or by contacting:

WestBow Press
A Division of Thomas Nelson & Zondervan
1663 Liberty Drive
Bloomington, IN 47403
www.westbowpress.com
1 (866) 928-1240

ISBN: 978-1-4908-8087-7 (sc)
ISBN: 978-1-4908-8088-4 (hc)
ISBN: 978-1-4908-8086-0 (e)

Library of Congress Control Number: 2015907939

Print information available on the last page.

WestBow Press rev. date: 5/21/2015

Contents

I Timothy

II Timothy

Titus

I Timothy

1

Overview and Outline of 1 Timothy

Who is the author? _____

When was the book written (indicate BC or AD)? _____

From what location was the book written? _____

What number is this book in the New Testament? _____

What number is this book in the canonical Bible? _____

Setting or location: _____

_____

_____

_____

_____

_____

What was the main purpose of this letter? _____

_____

What does the name *Timothy* mean? _____

_____

Who taught Timothy the Old Testament Scriptures during his childhood (2 Tim. 1:5; 3:15)? _____

Who was Timothy's father (Acts 16:1)? _____

What ethnicity or nationality was Timothy? _____

_____

Where was Timothy raised (Acts16:1–3)? _____

_____

What is the name of the collection of books of which 1 Timothy is the first book? _____

> Note: The city of Ephesus was known for accommodating the Greek god Artemis (Diana). It appears that there was trouble in the church because of some people who had been members of the church for a long time. These members were promoting false teachings (abstinence from marriage and from certain foods, ungodly interpretations of the Scriptures, materialism, false qualifications of leadership) and were causing turmoil, confusion, and anarchy, all of which led to disputes, division, and even withdrawal from the faith.

Book Blueprint

- Instructions concerning belief and false doctrine are found in 1 Timothy 1–3.
- Instructions for leadership and the man of God are found in 1 Timothy 4–6.

Major Arguments

Throughout our lives, we are subject to following rules and disciplines.[1] Therefore, there are always people who are trying to change the rules or policies for their own personal benefit. As Christians, we must be

---

[1] *Life Application Study Bible, New International Version*, Tyndale House Publishers, Inc. and Zondervan Publishing House, 1988, 1989, 1990, 1991.

aware of heresy and be ready to take a stand for what is right. We do this by knowing the Word of God for ourselves.

Prayer is an essential component of living a Christian life. People cannot build or increase their relationships with God without communication with God. Prayer is the avenue or instrument. Hence, it is important that we have the proper attitude toward our brothers and sisters—and most importantly, toward God—whether we are in private or in public.

As Christians, we become excited about our relationship with God, and we want to share and help others who are lost or in need to find the Lord. However, change comes about when we first look inside ourselves and become obedient to the Word for the glory of God, not for ourselves. This may entail the regular exercise of staying in spiritual shape through the study of God's Word, prayer, meditation, and everyday obedience.

The church is responsible for its members. When we minister and care for the church family, we are required to go beyond any plan and to be inclusive of our members of the body and the fellowship.

2

System of Belief: 1 Timothy 1

Chapter Blueprint

- Greeting (1:1–2)
- False doctrine (1:3–11)
- God's grace (1:12–17)
- The good fight (1:18–20)

Greeting

"Paul, an apostle of Christ Jesus by the command of God our Savior and of Christ Jesus our hope" (v. 1).

What are the identifying characteristics of an apostle (Mark 3:30)?

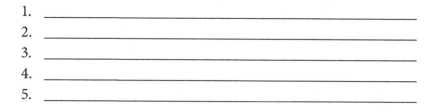

1. _____
2. _____
3. _____
4. _____
5. _____

📖

"To Timothy my true son in the faith: Grace, mercy and peace from God the Father and Christ our Lord" (v. 2).

To whom is the letter written? _____

Why is Timothy called the "true son"? _____

_____

What is different in the greeting to Timothy compared to the Epistles?

_____

What does "mercy" mean? _____

False Doctrine

"As I urged you when I went to Macedonia, stay there in Ephesus so that you may command certain men not to teach false doctrines any longer not to devote themselves to myths and endless genealogies. These promote controversies rather than God's work, which is by faith" (vv. 3–4).

What was Paul doing in Ephesus before he left for Macedonia (v. 3)?

_____

What was Timothy's charge in Ephesus (vv. 3–4)?

    1. _____

    2. _____

    3. _____

What is the problem with false doctrines (v. 4)? _____

_____

What may be a problem with church traditions? _____

_____

God's work is what type of act (v. 4)? _____

📖

"The goal of this command is love, which comes from a pure heart and a good conscience and a sincere faith. Some have wandered away from these and turned to meaningless talk" (vv. 5–6).

What can we deduce about the Ephesian church (v. 5)? _____

_____

Where does love come from (v. 5)?
1. _____
2. _____
3. _____

What caused some people to stray and turn to idle talk (v. 6)? _____

_____

_____

📖

"They want to be teachers of the law, but they do not know what they are talking about or what they so confidently affirm" (v. 7).

What is identified as the problem with some people and leaders in the church? _____

_____

_____

> The fear of the Lord is the beginning of wisdom,
> and the knowledge of the Holy One is understanding!
> —Proverbs 9:10

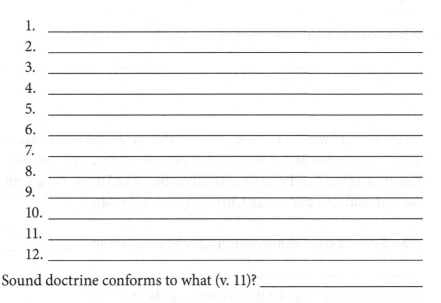

"We know that the law is good if one uses it properly" (v. 8).

What law is Paul referring to, and why is it good? _____

_____

"We also know that law is made not for the righteous but for lawbreakers and rebels, the ungodly and sinful, the unholy and irreligious; for those who kill their fathers or mothers, for murderers, for adulterers and perverts, for slave traders and liars and perjurers, and for whatever else is contrary to the sound doctrine that confirms to the glorious gospel of the blessed God, which he entrusted to me" (vv. 9–11).

The law is made for whom (vv. 9–10)?

1. _____
2. _____
3. _____
4. _____
5. _____
6. _____
7. _____
8. _____
9. _____
10. _____
11. _____
12. _____

Sound doctrine conforms to what (v. 11)? _____

_____

What does God entrust to us as Christians (v. 11)? _____

_____

God's Grace

"I thank Christ Jesus our Lord, who has given me strength, that he considered me faithful, appointing me to His service" (v. 12).

As Christians and as leaders, what should we continually do? _____
_____

What does it mean to "enable" or to give strength? _____
_____

For God to use us as positive teaching instruments, what must we be?
_____

What does "faithful" mean? _____
_____
_____
_____

Whose idea is it for someone to serve, and in what capacity? _____
_____

📖

"Even though I was once a blasphemer and a persecutor and a violent man, I was shown mercy because I acted in ignorance and unbelief. The grace of our Lord was poured out on me abundantly, along with the faith and love that are in Christ Jesus" (vv. 13–14).

Why did God show compassion/mercy to Paul (v. 13)? _____
_____

What is the grace that Paul was speaking about (v. 14)? _____
_____

"Abundantly" refers to what aspect of grace (v. 14)? _____
_____

What are "faith" and "love" (v. 14)? _____

📖

"Here is a trustworthy saying that deserves full acceptance: Christ Jesus came into the world to save sinners, of whom I am the worst. But for that very reason I was shown mercy so that in me, the worst of sinners, Christ Jesus might display His unlimited patience as an example for those who would believe on Him and receive eternal life" (vv. 15–16).

Why did Jesus come into the world (v. 15)? _____
_____

Why did Paul consider himself the worst (v. 15)? (See verse 13.) ____
_____

What is one of the reasons that Paul was saved by God (v. 16)? ____
_____
_____

📖

"Now to the King eternal, immortal, invisible, the only God, be honor and glory forever and ever. Amen" (v. 17).

This verse can be considered what? What type of utterances is this clause?

    1. _____
    2. _____
    3. _____

The Good Fight

"Timothy, my son, I give you this instruction in keeping with the prophecies once made about you, so that by following them you my fight the good fight, holding on to faith and a good conscience. Some have rejected these and so have shipwrecked their faith" (vv. 18–19).

What prophecies could Paul be referencing (v. 18)? (See 2 Tim. 2:3–4; 4:7.) _____

_____

_____

What is the reason to keep or honor the prophecies (vv. 18–19)? ___

_____

How can your faith be shipwrecked (v. 19)? _____

_____

Why did God, through Paul, use the term *shipwrecked* (v. 19)? _____

_____

📖

"Among them are Hymenaeus and Alexander, whom I have handed over to Satan to be taught not to blaspheme" (v. 20).

"Handed over to Satan" refers to what? _____

_____

What is the only way not to blaspheme? _____

3

Instructions for the Church: 1 Timothy 2

Chapter Blueprint

- Prayer (2:1–8)
- Women in the church (2:9–15)

Prayer

"I urge, then, first of all, that requests, prayers, intercession and thanksgiving be made for everyone" (v. 1).

Paul started this chapter with the words "I urge," or "I exhort." What does this mean? _____

_____

What are supplications or requests? _____

_____

Prayers consist of what? _____

_____

What is meant by "intercession"? _____

_____

Why is thanksgiving important? _____

_____

Was Paul laying out a formula for prayer? _____

_____

God, through Paul, stated that we should pray for whom? _____

_____

For whom do you pray *regularly*?

1. _____
2. _____
3. _____
4. _____
5. _____
6. _____
7. _____
8. _____
9. _____
10. _____

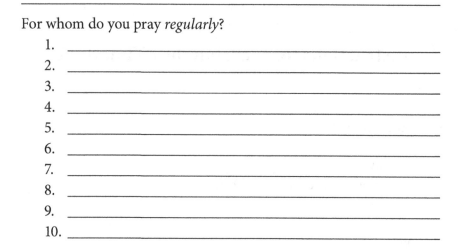

"For kings and all those in authority, that we may live peaceful and quiet lives in all godliness and holiness. This is good, and pleased God our Savior, who wants all men to be saved and to come to a knowledge of the truth" (vv. 2–4).

Who are the kings (v. 2)? _____

_____

Who are those in authority (v. 2)? _____

_____

What type of life is quiet and peaceful (v. 2)? _____

_____

What is the meaning of the phrase "in all godliness and holiness (honesty)" (v. 2)? _____

_____

How is God pleased (v. 2)? _____

_____

What appears to be one of the problems in both the church of Ephesus and today's church? _____

_____

_____

How did Paul refer to false teachers who promoted Gnosticism?

_____

God, our Savior, is represented or revealed in whom? _____

What is the desire of God (v. 4)? _____

_____

_____

According to Paul, who is outside God's grace and mercy? _____

_____

Is there a difference between God's will and God's desire? _____

_____

_____

📖

"For there is one God and one mediator between God and man, the man Christ Jesus, who gave Himself as a ransom for all men, the testimony given in its proper time" (vv. 5–6).

Who is the middleman or mediator between God and humans (v. 5)?

_____

_____

What does "mediator" mean (v. 5)? _____

_____

What did Jesus do for humankind (v. 6)? _____

_____

What does "ransom" mean (v. 6)? _____

_____

What is meant by the phrase "in due time" or "in its proper time" (v. 6)? _____

_____

What does "due time" or "proper time" have to do with prayer?

_____

_____

_____

Is prayer the desire or the will of God? _____

📖

"And for this purpose I was appointed a herald and an apostle, I am telling the truth, I am not lying, and a teacher of the true faith to the Gentiles" (v. 7).

How did Paul become a herald or preacher? _____

God blessed and anointed Paul as what?

1. _____
2. _____
3. _____

Why did Paul validate his credentials? _____

_____

_____

Paul was a teacher to what nation? _____

_____

📖

"I want men everywhere to lift up holy hands in prayer, without anger or disputing" (v. 8).

What appears to be the problem in the church regarding prayer?

_____

_____

What is a problem in today's church regarding prayer and worship?

_____

_____

Anger (wrath) and disputing (doubting) negates what? _____

_____

What did God say, through Paul, that your attitude must be when you pray? _____

_____

_____

_____

Women in the Church

> Note: Please take into consideration the culture, its customs regarding the family, and the structural hierarchy in the home, in public, and in church at that time.

What was another problem in the church? _____

_____

Does it matter how people clothe themselves in the church and around God's people? _____

_____

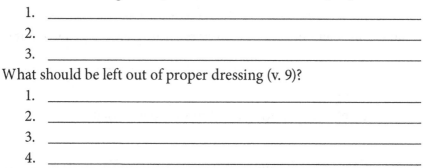

"I also want women to dress modestly, with decency and propriety, not with braided hair or gold or pearls or expensive clothes, but with good deeds appropriate for women who profess to worship God" (vv. 9–10).

God told us, through Paul, to dress in what manner (v. 9)?

1. _____
2. _____
3. _____

What should be left out of proper dressing (v. 9)?

1. _____
2. _____
3. _____
4. _____

"Good works" or "that which becomes women" refers to what (v. 10)?

_____

_____

"A woman should learn in quietness and full submission. I do not permit a woman to teach or to have authority over a man; she must be silent" (vv. 11–12).

How should a woman learn (v. 11)? _____

_____

"Silence" or "quietness" means what (v. 11)? _____

_____

"All subjection" or "full submission" means what (v. 11)? _____

_____

Why did Paul refuse to allow women to teach (v. 12)? _____

_____

_____

_____

📖

"For Adam was formed first, then Eve. And Adam was not the one deceived; it was the woman who was deceived and became a sinner" (vv. 13–14).

Who was deceived first (vv. 13–14)? _____

What is the significance of verses 13 and 14? _____

_____

_____

📖

"But women will be saved through childbearing, if they continue in faith, love and holiness with propriety" (v. 15).

Was Paul referring to a curse or a role given by God (v. 15)?

_____

_____

_____

_____

_____

Does this mean that all women *must* give birth in order to receive salvation? _____

_____

_____

How is this verse misused by taking a literal interpretation? _____

_____

_____

What is the purpose of Paul's comments toward men and women in the church? _____

_____

_____

4

Qualification of Church Leaders: 1 Timothy 3

Chapter Blueprint

- Criteria for elders (3:1–7)
- Criteria for deacons (3:8–13)
- Majestic mystery (3:14–16)

Criteria for Elders

"Here is a trustworthy saying: If anyone sets his heart on being a overseer, he desires a noble task" (v. 1).

What is a "faithful" or "trustworthy" saying (v. 1)? _____
_____

What does it mean to "set your heart" or have a "desire" (v. 1)? _____
_____

What is a bishop (v. 1)? _____
_____

Is this verse talking about the ordination or the office (v. 1)? _____
_____

📖

"Now the overseer must be above reproach, the husband of but one wife, temperate, self-controlled, respectable, hospitable, able to teach, not given to drunkenness, not violent but gentle, not quarrelsome, not a lover of money" (vv. 2–3).

To be blameless or above reproach means what (v. 2)? _____

_____

Can a single man, or a man married more once, become an elder (v. 2)? _____

_____

_____

What do the following terms and phrases mean (v. 2)?

Temperate _____

_____

Sober-minded (self-controlled) _____

_____

Good behavior (respectable) _____

_____

Hospitable _____

_____

Able to teach _____

Not given to wine (drunkenness) _____

_____

_____

Not violent _____

Not greedy (not a lover of money) _____

Not quarrelsome _____

📖

"He must mange his own family well and see that his children obey him with proper respect" (v. 4).

What does it mean to manage (rule) one's house well (v. 4)? _____

_____

Having children in submission means what (v. 4)? _____

_____

📖

"If anyone does not know how to manage his own family, how can he take care of God's church?" (v. 5).

What appears to be a problem in the church regarding new leaders

(v. 5)? _____

_____

_____

📖

"He must not be a recent convert, or he may become conceited and fall under the same judgment as the devil. He must also have a good reputation with outsiders, so that he will not fall into disgrace and into the devil's trap" (vv. 6–7).

What is a novice (v. 6)? _____

What is the plight of a novice who tries to be a leader (v. 7)? _____

_____

To keep from falling into disgrace (reproach) or the devil's trap

(snare), what must one have (v. 7)? _____

_____

Criteria for Deacons

"Deacons, likewise, are to be men worthy of respect, sincere, not indulging in much wine, and not pursuing dishonest gain" (v. 8).

What is a deacon? _____

_____

What are the four requirements of a deacon (v. 8)?

1. _____

2. _____

3. _____

4. _____

Are these four requirements for deacons also requirements for elders?

_____

📖

"They must keep hold of the deep truths of the faith with a clear conscience. They must first be tested; and then if there is nothing against them, let them serve as deacons" (vv. 9–10).

What is the "truth" or "mystery" of faith (v. 9)? _____

_____

What is a clear (pure) conscious (v. 9)? _____

_____

What must the church do before allowing people to serve as leaders (v. 10)? _____

_____

What is the practice for testing in your church or denomination?

_____

_____

When the testing is over, what must have been learned about the candidate (v. 10)? _____

_____

Can a deacon be married? _____

📖

"In the same way, their wives are to be women worthy of respect, not malicious talkers but temperate and trustworthy in everything" (v. 11).

In what manner should the wives behave (v. 11)?

1. _____
2. _____
3. _____
4. _____

📖

"A deacon must be the husband of but one wife and must manage his children and his household well. Those who have served well gain and excellent standing and great assurance in their faith in Christ Jesus" (vv. 12–13).

How many wives can a deacon have (v. 12)? _____

What other requirement is there for a deacon (v. 12)? _____

_____

What is the reward for good service as a leader (v. 13)? _____

_____

_____

Majestic Mystery

"Although I hope to come to you soon, I am writing you these instructions so that, if I am delayed, you will know how people ought to conduct themselves in God's household, which is the church of the living God, the pillar and foundation of the truth" (vv. 14–15).

Verse 14 is evidence of what (v. 14)? _____

_____

What is the reason or purpose for Paul's writing (v. 15)? _____

_____

The "house of God" is what (v. 15)?

    1. _____

    2. _____

    3. _____

Are these synonyms, or are they a description of the house of God (v. 15)? _____

_____

📖

"Beyond all question, the mystery of godliness is great: He appeared in a body, was vindicated by the Spirit, was seen by angels, was preached among the nations, was believed on in the world, was taken up in glory" (v. 16).

"Beyond all question" or "without controversy" means what (v. 16)?

_____

What is the "mystery of godliness" (v. 16)? _____

_____

"Manifested in flesh" means what (v. 16)? _____

_____

"Vindicated or justified by the Spirit" means what (v. 16)? _____

_____

How was Jesus seen by angels (v. 16)? _____

_____

What is meant by "preached among the nations" (v. 16)? _____

_____

What does "believed on" mean (v. 16)? _____

_____

"Received (taken) up in glory" indicates what (v. 16)? _____

_____

5

Great Apostasy: 1 Timothy 4

Chapter Blueprint

- Conscious abandonment (4:1–5)
- A good minister (4:6–11)
- Steadfast to the call (4:12–16)

Conscious Abandonment

"The Spirit clearly says that in later times some will abandon the faith and follow deceiving spirits and things taught by demons" (v. 1).

What are the "latter" days (v. 1)? _____

_____

Who makes the statement about the latter days (v. 1)? _____

_____

What will happen in the latter days (v. 1)?

1. _____
2. _____
3. _____

Who are deceiving spirits? _____

_____

What are the doctrines or teachings of demons? _____

_____

📖

"Such teachings come through hypocritical liars, whose consciences have been seared as with a hot iron" (v. 2).

Who are hypocritical liars (v. 2)? _____

What does it mean to have a conscience seared with a hot iron (4:2)?

_____

_____

_____

📖

"They forbid people to marry and order them to abstain from certain foods, which God created to be received with thanksgiving by those who believe and who know the truth" (v. 3).

What was being taught by false teachers (v. 3)?

    1. _____

    2. _____

God stated that foods should be received in what manner (v. 3)?

_____

Who should receive the foods (v. 3)? _____

_____

📖

"For everything God created is good, and nothing is to be rejected if it is received with thanksgiving, because it is consecrated by the word of God and prayer" (vv. 4–5).

What types of food are meant to be rejected (v. 4)? _____

_____

How does all food become acceptable (vv. 4–5)? _____

_____

How do we consecrate food today? _____

What does 1 Thessalonians 5:18 state about "thanks"? _____

_____

A Good Minister

"If you point these things out to the brothers, you will be a good minister of Christ Jesus, brought up in the truths of the faith and of the good teaching that you have followed" (v. 6).

How will you be a good minister (v. 6)? _____

_____

What are "these things" (v. 6)? _____

_____

What are the "truths" or "words" of faith (v. 6)? _____

📖

"Have nothing to do with godless myths and old wives' tale; rather train yourself to be godly" (v. 7).

What are we as Christians supposed to reject (v. 7)? _____

_____

How are Christians supposed to exercise or train themselves (v. 7)?

_____

📖

"For physical training is of some value, but godliness has value for all things, holding promise for both the present life and the life to come" (v. 8).

What good comes from physical training (v. 8)? _____

_____

What good comes from godliness (v. 8)? _____

_____

Where do you apply your godliness? _____

_____

Should one ignore physical/bodily exercise? _____

📖

"This is a trustworthy saying that deserves full acceptance (and for this we labor and strive) that we have put our hope in the living God, who is the Savior of all men, and especially of those who believe" (v. 9–10).

What is a faithful or trustworthy statement (v. 9)? _____

_____

What do believers labor over (v. 10)? _____

_____

How is Jesus the Savior of all men (v. 10)? _____

_____

Why does the Scripture state "especially of those who believe" (v. 10)?

_____

_____

Steadfast to the Call

"Command and teach these things. Don't let anyone look down on you because you are young, but set an example for the believers in speech, in life, in love, in faith and in purity" (v. 11–12).

What are all Christians called to do (v. 11)? _____

_____

What does "young" mean in this verse (v. 12)? _____

_____

How do you rise above those who try to despise you (v. 12)?

1. _____
2. _____
3. _____
4. _____
5. _____
6. _____

"Until I come, devote yourself to the public reading of Scripture, to preaching and to teaching. Do not neglect your gift, which was given y through a prophetic message when the body of elders laid their hands on you" (vv. 13–14).

In being steadfast, we should devote ourselves to what (v. 13)?

    1. _____

    2. _____

    3. _____

What should we not neglect (v. 14)? _____

What was the prophetic message or prophecy (v. 14)? _____

_____

Do believers today receive prophetic messages? _____

_____

When are hands laid on believers and on clergy (v. 14)? _____

_____

What is one of the jobs of the elders in the church (v. 14)?

_____

📖

"Be diligent in these matters; give yourself wholly to them, so that everyone may see your progress" (v. 15).

How do these things become a part of you (v. 15)? _____

_____

📖

"Watch your life and doctrine closely. Persevere in them, because if you do, you will save both yourself and your hearers" (v. 16).

What are you supposed to watch or heed (v. 16)? _____

_____

To whom does "hearers" refer? _____

_____

6

Advice about Church Members: 1 Timothy 5

Chapter Blueprint

- Showing respect (5:1–2)
- Honor widows and widowers (5:3–16)
- Honor elders and servants (5:17–25)

Showing Respect

"Do not rebuke an older man harshly, but exhort him as if he were your father. Treat younger men as brothers, older women as mothers, and younger women as sisters, with absolute purity" (vv. 1–2).

What does "rebuke" mean (v. 1)? _____

_____

What does "exhort" mean (v. 1)? _____

_____

Why treat an older person as if he or she were your parent (vv. 1–2)?

_____

_____

What does it mean to treat the younger as your brother or sister (vv. 1–2)? _____

_____

"With all purity" refers to what (v. 2)? _____

_____

Honor Widows and Widowers

"Give proper recognition to those widows who are really in need. But if a widow has children or grandchildren, these should learn first of all to put their religion into practice by caring for their own family and so repaying their parents and grandparents, for this is pleasing to God" (vv. 3–4).

What does it mean to honor or give proper recognition to widows

(v. 3)? _____

_____

What is pleasing and acceptable to God (v. 4)? _____

_____

📖

"The widow who is really in need and left all alone puts her hope in God and continues night and day to pray and to ask God for help. But the widow who lives for pleasure is dead even while she lives" (vv. 5–6).

A person who is without, needs to do what (v. 5)?

    1. _____

    2. _____

    3. _____

    4. _____

    5. _____

The widow who lives for pleasure is what (v. 6)? _____

How can a person be dead while being alive? _____

_____

📖

"Give the people these instructions, too, so that no one may be open to blame. If anyone does not provide for his relatives, and especially for his immediate family, he has denied the faith and is worse than an unbeliever" (vv. 7–8).

Why do you need to share these instructions (v. 7)? _____

_____

What is worse than an unbeliever (v. 8)? _____

_____

Whom in your family are you refusing to help? _____

_____

📖

"No widow may be put on the list of widows unless she is over sixty, has been faithful to her husband, and is well known for her good deeds, such as bringing up children, showing hospitality, washing the feet of the saints, helping those in trouble and devoting herself to all kinds of good deeds" (vv. 9–10).

Why must one be over sixty to be on the widow's list (v. 9)?

_____

To be on the widow's list, one must meet these qualifications (vv. 9–10):

    1. _____

    2. _____

    3. _____

What are the "good deeds" (v. 10)?

    1. _____

    2. _____

    3. _____

4. _____

5. _____

📖

"As for younger widows, do not put them on such a list. For when their sensual desires overcome their dedication to Christ, they want to marry. Thus, they bring judgment on themselves, because they have broken their first pledge. Besides, they get into the habit of being idle and going about from house to house. And not only do they become idlers, but also gossips and busybodies, saying things they ought not to" (vv. 11–13).

What could overcome dedication to Christ (v. 11)? _____

_____

What "pledge" or "first faith" is broken (v. 12)? _____

_____

What is the result of breaking the pledge (v. 12)? _____

_____

What do people who break their covenant with God do (v. 13)?

_____

_____

📖

"So I counsel younger widows to marry, to have children, to manage their homes and to give the enemy no opportunity for slander. Some have in fact already turned away to follow Satan" (vv. 14–15).

Paul counseled young widows to do what (v. 14)?

1. _____

2. _____

3. _____

4. _____

What have some widows or widowers done (v. 15)? _____

_____

📖

"If any woman who is a believer has widows in her family, she should help them and not let the church be burdened with them, so that the church can help those widows who are really in need" (v. 16).

What should a believer do for a widow in the family (v. 16)? _____

_____

Honor Elders and Servants

"The elders who direct the affairs of the church well are worthy of double honor, especially those whose work is preaching and teaching. For the Scripture 'Do not muzzle the ox while it is treading out the grain,' and 'The worker deserves his wages'" (vv. 17–18).

How should the elders who are in leadership roles be treated (v. 17)?

_____

_____

Why should they be given double honor (v. 17)? _____

_____

What about those who preach and teach (v. 17)? _____

_____

What happens if you muzzle the ox (v. 18)? _____

_____

Who deserves his wages (v. 18)? _____

Can you identify seven leaders in your church?

1. _____
2. _____
3. _____
4. _____
5. _____
6. _____
7. _____

"Do not entertain an accusation against an elder unless it is brought by two or three witnesses. Those who sin are to be rebuked publicly, so that the others may take warning" (vv. 19–20).

What takes two or three witnesses (v. 19)? _____

_____

Why are we told to rebuke believers publicly (v. 20)? _____

_____

What does Matthew 18:15–17 say about believers who sin? _____

_____

_____

"I charge you, in the sight of God and Christ Jesus and the elect angels to keep these instructions without partiality, and to do nothing out of favoritism" (v. 21).

Who are the elect angels (v. 21)? _____

_____

To "show partiality" means to do what (v. 21)? _____

_____

📖

"Do not be hasty in the laying on of hands, and do not share in the sins of others. Keep yourself pure" (v. 22).

Why should you not lay hands on hastily (v. 22)? _____

_____

📖

"Stop drinking only water, and use a little wine because of your stomach and your frequent illnesses" (v. 23).

Why did Paul tell Timothy not to drink the water (v. 23)? _____

_____

How does this water-versus-wine illustration teach us about leadership? _____

_____

📖

"The sins of some men are obvious, reaching the place of judgment ahead of them; the sins of others trail behind them. In the same way, good deeds are obvious, and even those that are not cannot be hidden" (v. 24–25).

What is verse 24 telling us about sins of leaders (v. 24)? _____

_____

What does the last verse say about good deeds (v. 25)? _____

_____

7

Man or Woman of God: 1 Timothy 6

Chapter Blueprint

- Respect overseers (6:1–2)
- Greed and contentment (6:3–10)
- Pursue righteousness (6:11–21)

Respect Overseers

"All you are under the yoke of slavery should consider their masters worthy of full respect, so that God's name and our teaching may not be slandered" (v. 1).

What is another interpretation of the Greek name for "slavery" (v. 1)?

_____

What is meant by "full respect" (v. 1)? _____

_____

What is the purpose of considering a master worthy (v. 1)? _____

_____

📖

"Those who have believing masters are not to show less respect for them because they are brothers. Instead, they are to serve them even better, because those who benefit from their service are believers, and dear to them. These are the things you are to teach and urge on them" (v. 2).

For whom should you show the least respect (v. 2)? _____

_____

What should you do for believing brothers (v. 2)? _____

_____

What should you teach to fellow believers, servants, and slaves (v. 2)?

_____

Greed and Contentment

"If anyone teaches false doctrines and does not agree to the sound instruction of our Lord Jesus Christ and to godly teaching, he is conceited and understands nothing. He has an unhealthy interest in controversies and quarrels about words that result in envy, strife, malicious talk, evil suspicious and constant friction between men of corrupt mind, who have been robbed of the truth and who think that godliness is a means to financial gain" (vv. 3–5).

Who is considered conceited (vv. 3–4)? _____

_____

What is another word for *conceit*? _____

What does a conceited or proud man know (v. 4)? _____

What is the problem with a conceited or proud person (v. 4)?

    1. _____

    2. _____

Bad words result in what (vv. 4–5)?

    1. _____

    2. _____

3. _____

4. _____

5. _____

What do corrupt men or corrupt minds think (v. 5)? _____

_____

📖

"But godliness with contentment is great gain. For we brought nothing into the world, and we can take nothing out of it" (vv. 6–7).

What is "great gain" (v. 6)? _____

_____

What does *contentment* mean? _____

_____

What have we brought into the world (v. 7)? _____

_____

What can we claim as ours? _____

_____

What do we take with us in death (v. 7)? _____

_____

📖

"But if we have food and clothing, we will be content with that. People who want to get rich fall into temptation and a trap and into many foolish and harmful desires that plunge men into ruin and destruction" (vv. 8–9).

What blessings should we be content with (v. 8)? _____

_____

What happens to people who want to get rich (v. 9)?

1. _____
2. _____
3. _____
4. _____

What do harmful desires do to men (v. 9)? _____

_____

📖

"For the love of money is a root of all kinds of evil. Some people, eager for money, have wondered from the faith and pierced themselves with many griefs" (v. 10).

The love of money is what (v. 10)? _____

Is money bad or good? _____

_____

What has happened to some people who seek money (v. 10)?

1. _____
2. _____

What has brought about your current condition? _____

_____

Pursue Righteousness

"But you, man of God, flee from all this, and pursue righteousness, godliness, faith, love, endurance and gentleness" (v. 11).

Who is "you" (v. 11)? _____

What is the "man of God" supposed to do (v. 11)? _____

_____

📖

"But you, man of God, flee from all this, and pursue righteousness, godliness, faith, love, endurance and gentleness. Fight the good fight of the faith. Take hold of the eternal life to which you were called when you made your good confession in the presence of many witnesses" (vv. 11–12).

What should the man of God do (vv. 11–12)?

1. _____   _____
   _____

2. _____   _____
   _____

3. _____   _____
   _____

4. _____   _____
   _____

5. _____   _____
   _____

6. _____   _____
   _____

7. _____   _____
   _____

8. _____   _____
   _____

Who are the "many witnesses" (v. 12)? _____

_____

📖

"In the sight of God, who gives life to everything, and of Christ Jesus, who while testifying before Pontius Pilate made the good confession, I charge you to keep this command without spot or blame until the appearing of our Lord Jesus Christ" (vv. 13–14).

What do God and Jesus have to do with confessions (v. 13)? _____

_____

_____

What commandment are you supposed to keep (v. 14)? _____

_____

_____

How are you supposed to keep the commandment (v. 14)? _____

_____

How long are you supposed to keep the commandment (v. 14)? ____

_____

📖

"Which God will bring about in His own time, God, the blessed and only Ruler, the King of kings and Lord of lords, who alone is immortal and who lives in unapproachable light, whom no one has seen or can see. To Him be honor and might forever, Amen" (vv. 15–16).

When will the appearing be (v. 15)? _____

_____

God is known as whom (v. 15)?

    1. _____

    2. _____

    3. _____

    4. _____

What is God (v. 16)?

    1. _____

    2. _____

What is "unapproachable light" (v. 16)? _____

_____

What should be given to God (v. 16)?

1. _____

_____

"Amen" means what (v. 16)? _____

_____

"Command those who are rich in this present world not to be arrogant nor to put their hope in wealth, which is so uncertain, but to put their hope in God, who richly provides us with everything for our enjoyment" (v. 17).

What should we command to the rich (v. 17)? _____

_____

What does God do (v. 17)? _____

_____

"Command them to do good, to be rich in good deeds, and to be generous and willing to share. In this way they will lay up treasures for themselves as a firm foundation for the coming age, so that they may take hold of the life that is truly life" (vv. 18–19).

We should also command "those who have" to do what (v. 18)?

1. _____
2. _____
3. _____
4. _____

What is the purpose of doing good (v. 19)? _____

_____

📖

"Timothy, guard what has been entrusted to your care. Turn away from godless chatter and the opposing ideas of what is falsely called knowledge, which some have professed and is so doing have wandered from the faith. Grace be with you" (vv. 20–21).

What should a leader do (v. 20)?

1. _____

2. _____

3. _____

Knowledge can cause what (v. 21)? _____

_____

_____

_____

_____

II Timothy

8

Overview and Outline of 2 Timothy

Who is the author: _____

When was the book written (indicate BC or AD)? _____

From what location was the book written? _____

What number is this book in the New Testament? _____

What number is this book in the canonical Bible? _____

Setting or location: _____

_____

_____

_____

_____

_____

What was the main purpose of this letter? _____

_____

What does the name *Timothy* mean? _____

_____

Who taught Timothy the Old Testament Scriptures during his childhood (2 Tim. 1:5; 3:15)?_____

_____

Who was Timothy's father (Acts 16:1)? _____

What ethnicity or nationality was Timothy? _____

_____

Where was Timothy raised? (Acts16:1–3)? _____

_____

What is the name of the collection of books of which 2 Timothy is the second book? _____

_____

Note: The city of Ephesus was known for accommodating the Greek god Artemis (Diana). It appears that there was trouble in the church because of some people who had been members of the church for a long time. These members were promoting false teachings (abstinence from marriage and from certain foods, ungodly interpretations of the Scriptures, materialism, false qualifications of leadership) and were causing turmoil, confusion, and anarchy, all of which led to disputes, division, and even withdrawal from the faith. This led to "institutional" concerns. Also Gnosticism (the belief that salvation is through knowledge) was prevalent within the culture of Asia Minor.

Book Blueprint

- The base of servanthood (2 Timothy 1–2)
- Rocky roads in servanthood (2 Timothy 3–4)

Major Arguments

As Christians, we are called to defend our faith, to stand up for our belief and way of life.[2] In order to be able to do this effectively, we have to know the truth, God's Word. That means being careful of the source of the Word. Thus, it is imperative that we stay away from those sources that twist God's Word for their own purposes or benefits.

Prayer is an essential component of living a Christian life. People cannot build or increase their relationship with God without communication with God. Prayer is the avenue or instrument. Hence, it is important that we have the proper attitude toward our brothers and sisters—and most importantly, toward God—whether we are in private or in public.

As Christians, we become excited about our relationship with God, and we want to share and help others who are lost or in need to find the Lord. However, change comes about when we first look inside ourselves and become obedient to the Word for the glory of God, not for ourselves. This may entail the regular exercise of staying in spiritual shape through the study of God's Word, prayer, meditation, and everyday obedience.

---

[2] *Life Application Study Bible, New International Version*, Tyndale House Publishers, Inc. and Zondervan Publishing House, 1988, 1989, 1990, 1991.

9

Perseverance: 2 Timothy 1

Chapter Blueprint

- Greeting (1:1–2)
- Faithfulness (1:3–7)
- No embarrassment   (1:8–12)
- Be steadfast (1:13–18)

Greeting

"Paul, an apostle of Christ Jesus by the will of God, according to the promise of life that is in Christ Jesus. To Timothy, my dear son: Grace, mercy and peace from God the Father and Christ Jesus our Lord" (vv. 1–2).

By what is Paul called an apostle (v. 1)? _____

_____

What is the difference between Paul's calling in this letter and his

stated calling in the first letter? _____

_____

What promise is Paul talking about (v. 1)? _____

_____

What is difference between Paul's greeting to Timothy in this letter and his greeting in the first letter? _____

_____

_____

Faithfulness

"I thank God, whom I serve, as my forefathers did, with a clear conscience, as night and day I constantly remember you in my prayers" (v. 3).

What is the first thing we should do (v. 3)? _____

Whom are we called to serve (v. 3)? _____

How are we supposed to thank God (v. 3)? _____

_____

What should we do night and day (v. 3)? _____

_____

📖

"Recalling your tears, I long to see you, so that I may be filled with joy" (v. 4).

What does it mean to recall or be mindful of someone's tears (v. 4)?

_____

Recalling or being mindful results in what (v. 4)? _____

_____

Explain a time when you remembered someone and it brought joy to you.

_____

_____

_____

_____

📖

"I have been reminded of your sincere faith, which first lived in our grandmother Lois and in your mother Eunice and, I am persuaded, now lives in you also. For this reason I remind you to fan into flame the gift of God, which is in you through the lying on of my hands" (vv. 5–6).

What now lives in Timothy (v. 5)? _____

What is faith (v. 5)? _____

How does one "fan the flame" or "stir up" the gift of God (v. 6)?

_____

_____

_____

📖

"For God did not give us a spirit of timidity, but a spirit of power, of love and of self-discipline" (v. 7).

What did God give us (v. 7)?

1. _____
2. _____
3. _____
4. _____

No Embarrassment

"So do not be ashamed to testify about our Lord, or ashamed of me his prisoner. But join with me in suffering for the gospel, by the power of God, who has saved us and called us to a holy life, not because of anything we have done but because of his own purpose and grace. This grace was give us in Christ Jesus before the beginning of time" (vv. 8–9).

What should you not be ashamed to do (v. 8)? _____

_____

Explain a situation in which you should have spoken for the Lord but didn't. _____

_____

_____

_____

_____

When and how often are you ashamed or embarrassed by other Christians? _____

_____

How can we endure suffering for God (v. 8)? _____

What has the power of God done (v. 9)? _____

The "power of God" acted for what reasons (v. 9)? _____

_____

When and from whom did you receive your grace (v. 9)? _____

_____

📖

"But it has now been revealed through the appearing of our Savior, Christ Jesus, who has destroyed death and has brought life and immortality to light through the gospel" (v. 10).

God's grace has been revealed through whom (v. 10)? _____

What has Jesus done (v. 10)?

1. _____
2. _____
3. _____

📖

"And of this gospel I was appointed a herald and an apostle and a teacher. That is why I am suffering as I am. Yet I am not ashamed, because I know whom I have believed, and am convinced that he is able to guard what I have entrusted to him for that day" (vv. 11–12).

Paul was appointed by God as what (v. 11)?

1. _____
2. _____
3. _____

Why was Paul suffering (v. 12)? _____

_____

What was Paul convinced or persuaded of (v. 12)? _____

_____

_____

Be Steadfast

"What you heard from me, keep as the pattern of sound teaching, with faith and love in Christ Jesus" (v. 13).

What is "sound teaching" or "sound words" (v. 13)? _____

_____

How does Paul state or do everything? _____

_____

How should we do everything we do? _____

_____

📖

"Guard the good deposit that was entrusted to you, guard it with the help of the Holy Spirit who lives in us" (v. 14).

What is the "good thing" or "the deposit" that we are to keep and guard (v. 14)? _____

_____

How are we supposed to guard or keep it (v. 14)? _____

_____

📖

"You know that everyone in the province of Asia has deserted me, including Phygelus and Hermogenes" (v. 15).

Who were Phygelus and Hermogenes (v. 15)? _____

_____

📖

"May the Lord show mercy to the household of Onesiphorus, because he often refreshed me and was not ashamed of my chains. On the contrary, when he was in Rome, he searched hard for me until he found me" (v. 16–17).

Why did Paul ask for a blessing on the house of Onesiphorus (v. 16)?

_____

_____

What must we do in order to have godly people around us (v. 17)?

_____

_____

📖

"May the Lord grant that he will find mercy from the Lord on that day! You know very well in how many ways he helped me in Ephesus" (v. 18).

What was the prayer of Paul (v. 18)? _____

What is "that day" (v. 18)? _____

_____

10

Strong in Grace: 2 Timothy 2

Chapter Blueprint

- Endure (2:1–13)
- Approved by God (2:14–21)
- Behavior (2:22–26)

Endure

"You then, my son, be strong in the grace that is in Christ Jesus. And the things you have heard me say in the presence of many witnesses entrust to reliable men who will also be qualified to teach others" (vv. 1–2).

How are we supposed to endure (v. 1)? _____

_____

A songwriter said, "It makes no difference what the problem. I can go to _____ in prayer" (v. 1).

Reliable Christian men and women should do what (v. 2)? _____

_____

📖

"Endure hardship with us like a good soldier of Christ Jesus. No one serving as a soldier gets involved in civilian affairs, he wants to please his commanding officer. Similarly, if anyone completes as an athlete, he does not receive the victor's crown unless he competes according to the rules" (vv. 3–5).

What does "good soldier" mean (v. 3)? _____

_____

Paul's use of the words *entangle* or *being involved* refers to what (v. 4)?

_____

_____

_____

In order to receive the crown, by what must you compete (v. 5)?

_____

_____

In order to receive the crown of life, what must you do? _____

_____

📖

"The hardworking farmer should be the first to receive a share of the crops. Reflect on what I am saying, for the Lord will give you insight into all this" (vv. 6–7).

What does "hardworking" mean (v. 6)? _____

_____

Who should be first to receive a share (v. 6)? _____

_____

📖

"Remember Jesus Christ, raised from the dead, descended from David. This is my gospel, for which I am suffering even to the point of being chained like a criminal. But God's word is not chained" (vv. 8–9).

In order to endure, what should we remember (v. 8)? _____

_____

What is meant by "God's word is not chained" (v. 9)? _____

_____

_____

📖

"Therefore I endure everything for the sake of the elect, that they too may obtain the salvation that is in Christ Jesus, with eternal glory" (v. 10).

Who are the "elect" (v. 10)? _____

_____

📖

"Here is a trustworthy saying: If we died with Him, we will also live with Him; If we endure, we will also reign with Him. If we disown Him, He will also disown us; If we are faithless, He will remain faithful, for He cannot disown Himself" (vv. 11–13).

What does it mean to die and live with Christ (v. 11)? _____

_____

What happens if we keep the faith, or endure (v. 12)? _____

_____

What happens if we fail or refuse to keep the faith v. 12)? _____

_____

What is verse 13 referring to (v. 13)? _____

_____

Approved by God

"Keep reminding them of these things. Warn them before God against quarrelling about words; it is of no value, and only ruins those who listen" (v. 14).

Striving, fighting, or quarreling about words is what (v. 14)? _____

_____

📖

"Do your best to present yourself to God as one approved, a workman who does not need to be ashamed and who correctly handles the word of Truth" (v. 15).

To whom should you show yourself approved (v. 15)? _____

_____

How does a workman become able to handle the Word of Truth (v. 15)? _____

_____

📖

"Avoid godless chatter, because those who indulge in it will become more and more ungodly. Their teaching will spread like gangrene. Among them are Hymenaeus and Philetus who have wandered away from the truth. They say that the resurrection has already taken place, and they destroy the faith of some" (vv. 16–18).

Godless chatter or idle babblings result in what (v. 16)? _____

_____

Godless chatter is compared to what (v. 17)? _____

Who were Hymenaeus and Philetus (v. 17)? (See 1 Timothy 1:20.)

_____

_____

What were the false teachers saying (v. 18)? _____

_____

What type of philosophical view says that matter is evil and spirit is good? _____

_____

📖

"Nevertheless, God's solid foundation stands firm, sealed with this inscription: 'The Lord knows those who are His', and 'Everyone who confesses the name of the Lord must turn away from wickedness'" (v. 19).

God's Word being "sealed" means what (v. 19)? _____

_____

Who must turn away from wickedness (v. 19)? _____

📖

"In a large house there are articles not only of gold and silver, but also of wood and clay; some are for noble purpose and some of ignoble. If a man cleanses himself from the later, he will be an instrument for noble purposes, made holy, useful to the Master and prepared to do any good work" (vv. 20–21).

The large or great house is a metaphor for what (v. 20)? _____

_____

How can a man become an instrument for good (v. 21)? _____

_____

Why are we prepared to do good works (v. 21)? (See Ephesians 2:10.)

_____

_____

Behavior

"Flee the evil desires of youth, and pursue righteousness, faith, love and peace, along with those who call on the Lord out of a pure heart" (v. 22).

God commands us to do what (v. 22)?

1. _____
2. _____
3. _____
4. _____
5. _____

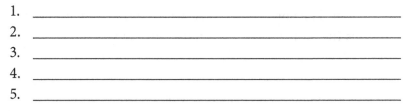

"Don't have anything to do with foolish and stupid arguments, because you know they produce quarrels" (v. 23).

What should we not do (v. 23)? _____

Arguments eventually lead to what (v. 23)? _____

📖

"And the Lord's servant must not quarrel; instead, he must be kind to everyone, able to teach, not resentful" (v. 24).

What must the Lord's servant or workman not do (v. 24)? _____

What should the Lord's servant be (v. 24)?

　　1. _____

　　2. _____

　　3. _____

📖

"Those who oppose him must gently instruct, in the hope that God will grant them repentance leading them to a knowledge of the truth and that they will come to their senses and escape from the trap of the devil, who has taken them captive to do his will" (v. 25–26).

What must the servant do to those who are against him (v. 25)?

_____

Why must the servant act with humility (v. 25–26)?

　　1. _____

　　2. _____

　　3. _____

　　4. _____

What has Satan done in opposition to believers (v. 26)? _____

_____

How often, how long, and when are you taken captive by the Devil?

_____

_____

_____

_____

11

Godlessness: 2 Timothy 3

Chapter Blueprint

- Terrible times and people (3:1–9)
- The Word and the man of God (3:10–17)

Terrible Times and People

"But mark this: There will be terrible times in the last days" (v. 1).

When will there be terrible times (v. 1)? _____

_____

When are the "last days" (v. 1)? _____

_____

"People will be lovers of themselves, lovers of money, boastful, proud, abusive, disobedient to their parents, ungrateful, unholy, without love, unforgiving, slanderous, without self-control, brutal, not lovers of the good, treacherous, rash, conceited, lovers of pleasure rather than lovers of God, having a form of godliness but denying its power. Have nothing to do with them" (vv. 2–5).

What will people be like in the last days (v. 2–4)?

1. _____
2. _____
3. _____
4. _____
5. _____
6. _____
7. _____
8. _____
9. _____
10. _____
11. _____
12. _____
13. _____
14. _____
15. _____
16. _____
17. _____
18. _____

What will people look like (v. 5)? _____

_____

How should Christian believers interact with these people (v. 5)?

_____

"They are the kind who worm their way into homes and gain control over weak willed women, who are loaded down with sins and are swayed by all kinds of evil desires, always learning but never able to acknowledge the truth" (vv. 6–7).

What is unique about godless people (v. 6)? _____

_____

"Weak-willed" or "gullible" women are recognized by what characteristics (v. 6–7)? _____

_____

How can one be always learning but unable to acknowledge the truth (v. 7)? _____

_____

_____

📖

"Just as Jannes and Jambres opposed Moses, so also these men oppose the truth, men of depraved minds, who, as far as the faith is concerned are rejected. But they will not get very far because, as in the case of those men, their folly will be clear to everyone" (vv. 8–9).

Who were Jannes and Jambres (v. 8)? _____

_____

What happens to people who reject the truth (v. 8)? _____

_____

When one acts foolishly, who knows about it (v. 9)? _____

_____

The Word and the Man of God

"You, however, know all about my teaching, my way of life, my purpose, faith patience, love, endurance, persecution, sufferings, what kinds of things happened to me in Antioch, Iconium and Lystra, the persecutions I endured. Yet the Lord rescued me from all of them" (vv. 10–11).

What did Timothy know about Paul (vv. 10–11)?

1. _____
2. _____
3. _____
4. _____
5. _____
6. _____
7. _____
8. _____
9. _____

What should leaders and Christians know about other Christians?

_____

_____

_____

_____

Where did Paul experience sufferings, afflictions, and persecutions (v. 11)?

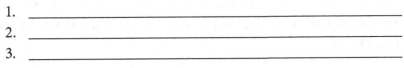

1. _____
2. _____
3. _____

What did the Lord do for Paul (v. 11)? _____

What will the Lord do for obedient believers? _____

_____

📖

"In fact, everyone who wants to live a godly life in Christ Jesus will be persecuted, while evil men and impostors will go from bad to worse, deceiving and being deceived" (vv. 12–13).

What will happen to all believers who follow Jesus (v. 12)? _____

_____

Name ten faces of persecution.

1. _____
2. _____
3. _____
4. _____
5. _____
6. _____
7. _____
8. _____
9. _____
10. _____

Evil people will experience what (v. 13)? _____

_____

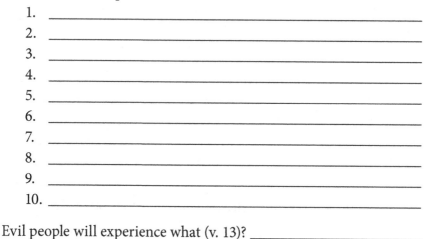

"But as for you, continue in what you have learned and have become convinced of, because you know those from whom you learned it, and how from infancy you have known the holy Scriptures, which are able to make you wise for salvation through faith in Christ Jesus" (vv. 14–15).

Christians must continue in what (v. 14)? _____

_____

What can the Holy Scriptures do for believers (v. 15)? _____

_____

"All Scripture is God-breathed and is useful for teaching, rebuking, correcting and training in righteousness, so that the man of God may be thoroughly equipped for every good work" (vv. 16–17).

Scripture, which is God's Word, comes from whom (v. 16)? _____

_____

All Scripture is good for what (v. 16)?

1. _____

2. _____

3. _____

4. _____

In this letter to Timothy, God states, through Paul, that the purpose of Scripture is for what (v. 17)? _____

_____

_____

The last sentence in chapter 3 was previously stated where else in 2 Timothy? _____

_____

The last sentence in chapter 3 sounds like what other Scripture in Ephesians 4? _____

_____

_____

12

Preach the Word: 2 Timothy 4

Chapter Blueprint

- Fulfill the ministry (4:1–5)
- The reward (4:6–8)
- Forsaken (4:9–16)
- God is my strength (4:17–18)
- Greetings (4:19–22)

Fulfill the Ministry

"In the presence of God and of Christ Jesus, who will judge the living and the dead, and in view of His appearing and His kingdom, I give you this charge" (v. 1).

Who will judge the living and the dead (v. 1)?

1. _____
2. _____

📖

"Preach the Word; be prepared in season and out of season; correct, rebuke and encourage, with great patience and careful instruction" (v. 2).

What is the command for all believers (v. 2)? _____

What should believers do with the Word (v. 2)?

1. _____
2. _____
3. _____
4. _____

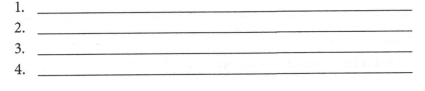

"For the time will come when men will not put up with sound doctrine. Instead, to suit their own desires, they will gather around them a great number of teachers to say what their itching ears want to hear. They will turn their ears away from the truth and turn aside to myths" (vv. 3–4).

In time, what will people refuse to do (v. 3)? _____

In time, what will people do (v. 3–4)?

1. _____
   _____
2. _____
3. _____

"But you, keep your head in all situations, endure hardship, do the work of an evangelist, discharge all the duties of your ministry" (v. 5).

God demands that believers do what (v. 5)?

1. _____
2. _____
3. _____
4. _____

What does it mean to be "watchful" or to "keep your head" (v. 5)?

_____

_____

Why must Christians endure hardships and afflictions?

_____

_____

What is the work of an evangelist (v. 5)? _____

_____

The Reward

"For I am already being poured out like a drink offering, and a time has come for my departure. I have fought the good fight, I have finished the race, I have kept the faith" (vv. 6–7).

What is or was a drink offering (v. 6)? (See Numbers 15:1–16.)

_____

_____

What should the lives of believers be? _____

To accomplish your purpose on earth, what must you do (v. 7)?

1. _____

    What does this mean? _____

    _____

2. _____

    What does this mean? _____

    _____

3. _____

    What does this mean? _____

    _____

"Now there is in store for me the crown of righteousness, which the Lord, the righteous judge, will award to me on that day, and not only to me, but also to all who have longed for His appearing" (v. 8).

What is the reward of the workman (v. 8)? _____

_____

Who is the Lord (v. 8)? _____

Whom will Christ Jesus award (v. 8)? _____

_____

Forsaken

"Do your best to come to me quickly, for Demas, because he loved this world, has deserted me and has gone to Thessalonica. Crescens has gone to Galatia,, and Titus to Dalmatia. Only Luke is with me. Get Mark and bring him with you, because he is helpful to me in my ministry. I sent Tychicus to Ephesus. When you come, bring the cloak that I left with Carpus at Troas, and my scrolls, especially the parchments" (vv. 9–13).

How should one take care of business (v. 9)? _____

Demas was known for what (v. 10)? _____

Name five times when you felt deserted and alone.

1. _____
2. _____
3. _____
4. _____
5. _____

Who was the only person with Paul (v. 11)? _____

Why do you think Paul asked for Mark (v. 11)? _____

_____

Why did Tychicus go to Ephesus (v. 12)? _____

_____

When life's circumstances have imprisoned us, what should we do (v. 13)? _____

_____

_____

📖

"Alexander the metalworker did me a great deal of harm. The Lord will repay him for what he has done. You too should be on your guard against him, because he strongly opposed our message" (vv. 14–15).

Who repays for evil done to others (v. 14)? _____

Why do Christians need to be aware of their surroundings (v. 15)?

_____

_____

_____

📖

"At my first defense, no one came to my support, but everyone deserted me. May it not be held against them" (v. 16).

Who came to help Paul at his first defense (v. 16)? _____

Describe a time when you stood by and did nothing when people accused someone.

_____

_____

_____

_____

_____

God Is My Strength

"But the Lord stood at my side and gave me strength, so that through me the message might be fully proclaimed and all the Gentiles might hear it. And I was delivered from the lion's mouth" (v. 17).

Who stood at Paul's side when he was in need (v. 17)? _____

Scripture states, "I will never _____ you or

_____ you."

What does Philippians 4:19 state? _____

_____

What does Philippians 4:13 state? _____

_____

God gave Paul the strength to do what (v. 17)? _____

_____

Who or what is the "lion's mouth" (v. 17)? _____

_____

📖

"The Lord will rescue me from every evil attack and will bring me safely to His heavenly kingdom. To Him be glory forever and ever. Amen" (v. 18).

What will the Lord do for His people/children (v. 18)?

    1. _____

    2. _____

Glory goes to whom (v. 18)? _____

What does "amen" mean (v. 18)? _____

_____

Greetings

"Greet Priscilla and Aquila and the household of Onesiphorus. Erastus stayed in Corinth, and I left Trophimus sick in Miletus. Do your best to get here before winter. Eubulus greets you, and so do Pudens, Linus, Claudia and all the brothers" (vv. 19–21).

Who were Priscilla and Aquila (v. 19)? _____

Who were Eratus and Trophimus (v. 19)? _____

"The Lord be with your spirit. Grace be with you" (v. 22).

Paul always ended his letters with what type of blessing (v. 22)?

_____

_____

_____

_____

13

Overview and Outline of Titus

Who is the author? _____

When was the book written (indicate BC or AD)? _____

From what location was the book written? _____

What number is this book in the New Testament? _____

What number is this book in the canonical Bible? _____

The book of Titus, belongs to what Bible collection of books? _____

_____

Setting or location: _____

_____

_____

_____

_____

What was the main purpose of this letter? _____

_____

What was Titus's ethnicity? _____

_____

> Note: Crete was known to be one of the largest islands in the Mediterranean body of water just south of the Aegean Sea. False teachers and Judaizers were among the people presenting opposition. The book of Titus emphasizes and upholds the election of believers, the atonement and deity of Christ, the power of the Holy Spirit to renew and revive believers, and the saving grace of our Savior, Jesus Christ, who is God.

Book Blueprint

- Leadership in the church (Titus 1)
- Characteristics of a healthy church (Titus 2)
- Living in society (Titus 3)

Major Arguments

Society has a history of looking to tangible things, material things, things that are seen but are temporary.[3] As Christians, we know and understand that salvation only comes through trusting and having faith in Jesus Christ. Hence, there must be a transformation that takes place, which comes by following the teachings of Jesus. As a result, His Word makes over our lives and places us in a position whereby we can serve Him in a manner that is pleasing and acceptable to God.

Being a leader is not a task for every person. True leadership demands special qualities that stem from the inner essence of our being. Thus, it is not something we can turn off and on. Leadership qualities finds their fiber or character during all hours of the day. What a person does at home relates to his ability and fitness to lead or serve in the church.

---

[3] *Life Application Study Bible, New International Version*, Tyndale House Publishers, Inc. and Zondervan Publishing House, 1988, 1989, 1990, 1991.

In order for the church to grow with balance, church teachings must relate to people of all ages and must permeate all groups. As Christians, we are called to step up and live a good life that coincides with the doctrines and teachings of the Bible, one that shows evidence of our faith in God and Jesus Christ.

Society and its rules are not always in sync with the church. But that doesn't mean we should drop one and adopt the other. As Christians, we have a duty to be obedient to the laws of the land. This includes working honestly while being a lighthouse, a reflection of Christ's love that is in us.

14

Leadership in the Church: Titus 1

Chapter Blueprint

- Greeting (1:–4)
- Qualified overseers (1:5–9)
- The charge for elders (1:10–16)

Greeting

"Paul, a servant of God and an apostle of Jesus Christ for the faith of God's elect and the knowledge of the truth that leads to godliness" (v. 1).

Paul was a servant and apostle for whom (v. 1)? _____

_____

What is the faith and knowledge of truth (v. 1)? _____

_____

"A faith and knowledge resting on the hope of eternal life, which God, who does not lie, promised before the beginning of time" (v. 2).

Why is God trustworthy (v. 2)? _____

When did God promise eternal life (v. 2)? _____

📖

"And at His appointed season he brought His word to light through the preaching entrusted to me by the command of God our Savior" (v. 3).

When did God bring His Word to light (v. 3)? _____

In what manner has God made His Word known (v. 3)? _____

_____

📖

"To Titus, my true son in our common faith: Grace and peace from God the Father and Christ Jesus our Savior" (v. 4).

What was the relationship between Paul and Titus (v. 4)? _____

_____

What was the blessing or greeting from Paul (v. 4)? _____

_____

Qualified Overseers

"The reason I left you in Crete was that you might straighten out what was left unfinished and appoint elders in every town, as I directed you" (v. 5).

Why did Paul leave Titus in Crete (v. 5)? _____

_____

What was happening in Crete that needed to be straightened out or set in order (v. 5)? _____

_____

What other duty was Titus to carry out (v. 5)? _____

"An elder must be blameless, the husband of but one wife, a man whose children believe and are not open to the charge of being wild and disobedient" (v. 6).

What are the requirements for being an elder or leader in the church (v. 6)?

1. _____
2. _____
3. _____

"Since an overseer is entrusted with God's work, he must be blameless, not overbearing, not quick-tempered, not given to drunkenness, not violent, not pursuing dishonest gain. Rather he must be hospitable, one who loves what is good, who is self-controlled, upright, holy and disciplined. He must hold firmly to the trustworthy message as it has been taught, so that he can encourage others by sound doctrine and refute those who oppose it" (vv. 7–9).

What is the difference between an *overseer* and an *elder* (vv. 6–7)?

_____

_____

What are the requirements for being an overseer (vv. 7–9)?

1. _____
2. _____
3. _____
4. _____
5. _____
6. _____
7. _____
8. _____
9. _____

10. _____

11. _____

12. _____

13. _____

Why must an overseer hold on to the Word as taught (v. 9)? _____

_____

The Charge for Elders

"For there are many rebellious people, mere talkers and deceivers, especially those of the circumcision group" (v. 10).

What is the attitude of many people within and outside of the church (v. 10)? _____

_____

What kinds of people are in the church (v. 10)?

1. _____

2. _____

3. _____

Who were part of the "circumcision group" (v. 10)? _____

What did Judaizers believe and teach? _____

"They must be silenced, because they are ruining whole households by teaching things they ought not to teach, and that for the sake of dishonest gain" (v. 11).

What should be done to rebellious people (v. 11)? _____

_____

Rebellious people are known for doing what (v. 11)? _____

_____

_____

📖

"Even one of their own prophets has said, 'Cretans are always liars, evil brutes, lazy gluttons.' This testimony is true. Therefore, rebuke them sharply, so that they will be sound in the faith and will pay no attention to Jewish myths or to the commands of those who reject the truth" (v. 12–14).

How did the people of Crete think of themselves (v. 12)? _____

_____

Why should the church rebuke rebellious people (vv. 13–14)? _____

_____

_____

📖

"To the pure, all things are pure, but to those who are corrupted and do not believe, nothing is pure. In fact, both their minds and consciences are corrupted. They claim to know God, but by their actions they deny Him. They are detestable, disobedient and unfit for doing anything good" (vv. 15–16).

What is the difference between the "pure" and the "corrupt" (defiled) (v. 15)? _____

What do the corrupt or defiled do (v. 16)?

    1. _____

    2. _____

What is the problem with the corrupt or defiled (v. 16)? _____

_____

15

Characteristics of a Healthy Church: Titus 2

Chapter Blueprint

- Teach and encourage (2:1–10)
- Say no (2:11–15)

Teach and Encourage

"You must teach what is in accord with sound doctrine. Teach the older men to be temperate, worthy of respect, self-controlled, and sound in faith, in love and in endurance" (vv. 1–2).

What should the church, church leaders, and believers teach (v. 1)?

_____

_____

What should the older men be taught to do (v. 2)?
1. _____
2. _____
3. _____
4. _____

How should the older men be taught (v. 2)? _____

_____

"Likewise, teach the older women to be reverent in the way they live, not to be slanderers or addicted to much wine, but to teach what is good. Then they can train the younger women to love their husbands and children, to be self-controlled and pure, to be busy at home, to be kind, and to be subject to their husbands, so that no one will malign the word of God" (vv. 3–5).

What should the older women be taught to be (v. 3)?

1. _____
2. _____
3. _____
4. _____

What should the older women train the younger women to do (vv. 4–5)?

1. _____
2. _____
3. _____
4. _____
5. _____

Why should we train each other in these disciplines (v. 5)? _____

_____

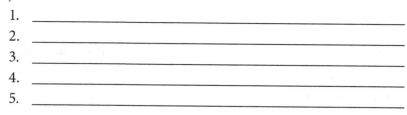

"Similarly, encourage the young men to be self-controlled. In everything set them an example by doing what is good. In your teaching show integrity, seriousness and soundness of speech that cannot be condemned, so that those who oppose you may be ashamed because they have nothing bad to say about us" (vv. 6–8).

What should the church and leaders encourage young men to be (v. 6)? _____

How can believers set an example (v. 7)? _____

When teaching, what should believers display (vv. 7–8)?

    1. _____

    2. _____

    3. _____

Why should they teach in this manner (v. 8)? _____

_____

"Teach slaves to be subject to their masters in everything, to try to please them, not to talk back to them, and not to steal from them, but to show that they can be fully trusted, so that in every way they will make the teaching about God our Savior attractive" (vv. 9–10).

What should slaves or bondservants be taught to be (v. 9)? _____

_____

What should slaves or bondservants not do (v. 9)? _____

_____

What is the purpose for submitting in everything (v. 10)? _____

_____

Say No

"For the grace of God that brings salvation has appeared to all men. It teaches us to say 'No' to ungodliness and worldly passions, and to live self-controlled, upright and godly lives in this present age" (vv. 11–12).

What does the grace of God bring (v. 11)? _____

What is grace? _____

What has the grace of God done (v. 11)? _____

What does the grace of God teach us (v. 12)?

1. _____
2. _____
3. _____
4. _____
5. _____

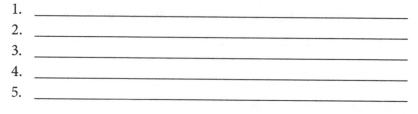

"While we wait for the blessed hope, the glorious appearing of our great God and Savior, Jesus Christ, who gave Himself for us to redeem us from all wickedness and to purify for Himself a people that are His very own, eager to do what is good" (vv. 13–14).

What is the blessed hope (v. 13)? _____

_____

What did Jesus Christ do for us (v. 14)? _____

Why did Jesus give of Himself (v. 14)? _____

_____

_____

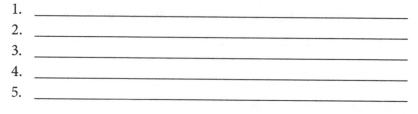

"These, then are the things you should teach. Encourage and rebuke with all authority. Do not let anyone despise you" (v. 15).

What are leaders, the church, and believers supposed to teach (v. 15)?

_____

_____

What authority are you to encourage and rebuke (v. 15)? _____

_____

What message is conveyed by the last sentence about despising (v. 15)?

_____

_____

_____

16

Living in Society: Titus 3

Chapter Blueprint

- Doing good (3:1–8)
- Avoiding conflict and discord (3:9–11)
- Final comments (3:12–15)

Doing Good

"Remind the people to be subject to rulers and authorities, to be obedient, to be ready to do whatever is good, to slander no one, to be peaceable and considerate, and to show true humility toward all men" (v. 1–2).

What should we as Christians remind ourselves and others (vv. 1–2)?

1. _____
2. _____
3. _____
4. _____
5. _____
6. _____

📖

"At one time we too were foolish, disobedient, deceived and enslaved by all kinds of passions and pleasures. We lived in malice and envy, being hated and hating on another" (v. 3).

Nonbelievers and the corrupt, or defiled, were foolish in doing what (v. 3)?

1. _____
2. _____
3. _____

How do the foolish live (v. 3)? _____

_____

📖

"But when the kindness and love of God our Savior appeared, He saved us, not because of righteous things we had done, but because of His mercy. He saved us through the washing of rebirth and renewal by the Holy Spirit, whom He poured out on us generously through Jesus Christ our Savior" (vv. 4–5).

What appeared (v. 4)? _____

What should appear in our lives and be evident to others? _____

_____

What did our Savior do and why (v. 5)? _____

_____

What are the Beatitudes? _____

_____

Where can one find the Beatitudes? _____

_____

What do the Beatitudes have to say about mercy? _____

_____

How did Jesus save us (v. 5)? _____

_____

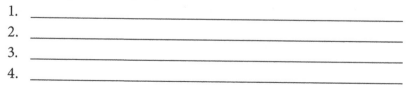

"So that, having been justified by His grace, we might become heirs having the hope of eternal life. This is a trustworthy saying. And I want you to stress these things, so that those who have trusted in God may be careful to devote themselves to doing what is good. These things are excellent and profitable for everyone" (vv. 7–8).

Christians are justified by what (v. 7)? _____

As heirs with Christ, what is our hope (v. 7)? _____

A trustworthy saying is what kind of saying (v. 8)? _____

_____

Those who trust in God must devote themselves to what (v. 8)?

_____

_____

Avoiding Conflict and Discord

"But avoid foolish controversies and genealogies and arguments and quarrels about the law, because these are un profitable and useless" (v. 9).

What should you avoid (v. 9)

1. _____
2. _____
3. _____
4. _____

What is the result of conflict and discord (v. 9)? _____

_____

"Warn a divisive person once, and then warn him a second time. After that, have nothing to do with him. You may be sure that such a man is warped and sinful; he is self-condemned" (vv. 10–11).

What should believers do with a divisive person (v. 10)? _____

_____

What is the problem with a divisive person (v. 11)?

1. _____

2. _____

3. _____

Final Comments

"As soon as I send Artemas or Tychicus to you, do your best to come to me at Nicopolis, because I have decided to winter there. Do everything you can to help Zenas the lawyer and Apollos on their way and see that they have everything they need" (vv. 12–13).

What should we do for our fellow brothers and sisters in Christ (v. 12–13)? _____

_____

_____

"Our people must learn to devote themselves to doing what is good, in order that they may provide for daily necessities and not live unproductive lives" (v. 14).

Christians must devote themselves to what (v. 14)? _____

Why must one do good (v. 14)? _____

_____

_____

📖

"Everyone with me sends you greetings. Greet those who love us in the faith. Grace be with you all" (v. 15).

What was the final wish of Paul to Titus and the churches in Crete (v. 15)? _____

The last sentence is what (v. 15)? What type of actions are evoked by the last clause

    1. _____

    2. _____

    3. _____

    4. _____